EMOJIS

New Number and Logic Puzzles

T0163123

How it all began

In May 2000 I had an accident, falling from a ladder, and needed 5 months off work.

Boredom soon set in and as I love numbers I decided to try and devise some number puzzles.

I put three rows of numbers from 1 to 9 on a spreadsheet. I then inserted a formula that added the middle number to the top and bottom numbers and printed out the result.

I then erased all the numbers just leaving the top and bottom totals then by using addition tried to reinstate the correct numbers.

It was then that I had that "Eureka" moment, realising that because the middle row was common to both sums, up and down, it would need logic to place the correct combinations in the right order, and so my ZYGO puzzle was born!

I had a new addictive hobby.

In the years that followed I devised many new number puzzles and compiled computer programs that generated them automatically.

A year or two ago, I thought I would try and get some puzzles published and contacted Andrew Griffin at Tarquin who decided to publish 6 puzzle books for everyone to enjoy.

EMOJIS

New Number and Logic Puzzles

Les Page

Tarquin

Publisher's Note

If you have enjoyed this Emojis book and want to get someone else like a child into them - there is a Starter version of Emojis. This and 4 other books are described below - fuller details on www.tarquingroup.com. Enjoy!

Samples of some of the puzzles in other books can be found at the back of this book.

Les Page has asserted his right to be identified as the author of this work under the Copyright, Designs and Patents Act 1988.

All rights reserved. No part of this publication may be reproduced, stored any means in a retrieval system, or transmitted in any form or by any means, electronic, mechanical, photocopying, recording or otherwise without the prior permission of the copyright owner.

© Les Page 2020
ISBN UK (Book) 978-1-913565-00-8
ISBN (EBook) 978-1-913565-01-5
Designed and Printed in the UK

Tarquin
Suite 74, 17 Holywell Hill
St Albans AL1 1DT
UK
www.tarquingroup.com

Contents

Puzzles 1–23

Start on page 1 overleaf. Solutions to each are on reverse side of the puzzle page.

Bonus Puzzles

On page 51–60 there are some preview puzzles from other books in the series. These books are set out below. If you enjoy a particular puzzle from the bonuses, get the whole book from your usual bookseller or from www.tarquingroup.com

The Compendium
Book ISBN 9781913565060
Ebook ISBN 9781913565077

Nightmare Blocks
Book ISBN 9781913565022
Ebook ISBN 9781913565039

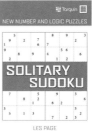

Solitary Sudoku
Book ISBN 9781913565046
Ebook ISBN 9781913565053

The Starter Books

Emojis - The Starter Book
Book ISBN 9781913565084
Ebook ISBN 9781913565091

Nightmare Blocks -
The Starter Book
Book ISBN 9781913565107
Ebook ISBN 9781913565114

EMOJIS

PUZZLE 1

15 EMOJIS have different numerical values. Put the values in the puzzle grid to agree the sum totals horizontally, vertically and diagonally.

↓ = ∩ Enter values when worked out   Yellow boxes are "given" values

		=	
1 x		=	
2 x	☺	=	6
1 x	☞	=	
2 x	❖	=	
2 x	✈	=	
2 x	✋	=	
2 x	☹	=	
2 x	☺	=	10
1 x	👍	=	15
2 x	💣	=	21
2 x	⌘	=	
1 x	☝	=	12
2 x	⚑	=	
1 x	👎	=	
2 x	☠	=	

↘	↓	↓	↓	↓	↓	↙
→	✈	☠	✋	☞	✈	56
→	☠	☺	✋	👍	☞	50
→	☹	⚑	☺	⚑	☺	57
→	❖	💣	❖	☝	☺	65
→	⌘	⌘	☹	👎	💣	62
57	48	52	66	70	54	62

↘	↓	↓	↓	↓	↓	↙
→						56
→		10		15		50
→			6			57
→		21		12		65
→						62
57	48	52	66	70	54	62

Cross out numerical values when placed

✗

2
4
5
6
9
10
11
12
13
14
15
16
17
20
21

Solution Overleaf

© Les Page 2020   ISBN 9781913565008   For more www.tarquingroup.com

EMOJIS

SOLUTION 1

Emoji grid (top):

↘	↓	↓	↓	↓	↓	↙
→	✈	☠	🖐	☞	✈	56
→	☠	☺	🖐	👍	☞	50
→	☹	⚑	☺ (neutral)	⚑	☺ (neutral)	57
→	❖	💣	❖	☝	☺	65
→	⌘	⌘	☹	👎	💣	62
57	48	52	66	70	54	62

Number grid (bottom):

↘	↓	↓	↓	↓	↓	↙
→	13	5	16	9	13	56
→	5	10	16	15	4	50
→	17	14	6	14	6	57
→	11	21	11	12	10	65
→	2	2	17	20	21	62
57	48	52	66	70	54	62

Key:

Symbol		Value
⌘	=	2
☞	=	4
☠	=	5
☺ (neutral)	=	6
🖝	=	9
☺	=	10
❖	=	11
☝	=	12
✈	=	13
⚑	=	14
👍	=	15
🖐	=	16
☹	=	17
👎	=	20
💣	=	21

© Les Page 2020   ISBN 9781913565008

PUZZLE 2

15 EMOJIS have different numerical values. Put the values in the puzzle grid to agree the sum totals horizontally, vertically and diagonally.

↓ = ⤴ Enter values when worked out   Yellow boxes are "given" values

Cross out numerical values when placed

1 x	👉	=	
2 x	😐	=	
1 x	👉	=	
2 x	✦	=	
2 x	✈	=	
2 x	✋	=	9
2 x	☹	=	6
2 x	☺	=	
1 x	👍	=	
2 x	💣	=	
2 x	⌘	=	18
1 x	☝	=	14
2 x	🏳	=	
1 x	👎	=	
2 x	☠	=	1

↘	↓	↓	↓	↓	↓	↙
→	☺	👎	✋	💣	😐	58
→	☺	☝	✈	☠	✦	50
→	👉	👍	⌘	✦	😐	73
→	⌘	✋	☠	☹	🏳	51
→	✈	🏳	💣	☹	👉	51
44	82	57	49	39	56	65

↘	↓	↓	↓	↓	↓	↙
→						58
→		14		1		50
→			18			73
→		9		6		51
→						51
44	82	57	49	39	56	65

Cross out numerical values when placed

1
2
5
6
7
9
10
11
14
15
16
17
18
19
20

Solution Overleaf

© Les Page 2020   ISBN 9781913565008   For more www.tarquingroup.com

SOLUTION 2

↘	↓	↓	↓	↓	↓	↙
→	☺	👎	🖐	💣	😐	58
→	☺	☝	✈	☠	✤	50
→	👉	👍	⌘	✤	😐	73
→	⌘	🖐	☠	☹	🏳	51
→	✈	🏳	💣	☹	👉	51
44	82	57	49	39	56	65

↘	↓	↓	↓	↓	↓	↙
→	20	2	9	16	11	58
→	20	14	5	1	10	50
→	19	15	18	10	11	73
→	18	9	1	6	17	51
→	5	17	16	6	7	51
44	82	57	49	39	56	65

☠	=	1
👎	=	2
✈	=	5
☹	=	6
👉	=	7
🖐	=	9
✤	=	10
😐	=	11
☝	=	14
👍	=	15
💣	=	16
🏳	=	17
⌘	=	18
👉	=	19
☺	=	20

© Les Page 2020   ISBN 9781913565008

PUZZLE 3

15 EMOJIS have different numerical values. Put the values in the puzzle grid to agree the sum totals horizontally, vertically and diagonally.

Cross out numerical values when placed

↓ = ↻ Enter values when worked out   Yellow boxes are "given" values

1 x	🐦	=	
2 x	😀	=	
1 x	☞	=	7
2 x	❖	=	6
2 x	✈	=	
2 x	✋	=	
2 x	☹	=	
2 x	☺	=	
1 x	👍	=	
2 x	💣	=	5
2 x	⌘	=	11
1 x	☝	=	
2 x	🚩	=	2
1 x	👎	=	
2 x	☠	=	

↘	↓	↓	↓	↓	↓	↙
→	☝	☺	😀	👍	😐	54
→	✋	⌘	☠	🚩	☺	62
→	☹	⌘	❖	✈	👎	44
→	☠	💣	✈	☞	🚩	37
→	☞	💣	☹	❖	✋	55
50	65	45	56	22	64	41

↘	↓	↓	↓	↓	↓	↙
→						54
→		11		2		62
→			6			44
→		5		7		37
→						55
50	65	45	56	22	64	41

1
2
3
4
5
6
7
9
11
13
15
16
18
19
20

Solution Overleaf

© Les Page 2020   ISBN 9781913565008   For more www.tarquingroup.com

SOLUTION 3

↘	↓	↓	↓	↓	↓	↙
→	☝	☺	😐	👍	😀	54
→	🖐	⌘	☠	🏳	☺	62
→	😞	⌘	❖	✈	👎	44
→	☠	💣	✈	👉	🏳	37
→	👉	💣	😞	❖	🖐	55
50	65	45	56	22	64	41

☝	=	1
🏳	=	2
✈	=	3
👍	=	4
💣	=	5
❖	=	6
👉	=	7
😞	=	9
⌘	=	11
☺	=	13
👎	=	15
🖐	=	16
😐	=	18
👉	=	19
☠	=	20

↘	↓	↓	↓	↓	↓	↙
→	1	13	18	4	18	54
→	16	11	20	2	13	62
→	9	11	6	3	15	44
→	20	5	3	7	2	37
→	19	5	9	6	16	55
50	65	45	56	22	64	41

© Les Page 2020   ISBN 9781913565008

EMOJIS

LEVEL H

PUZZLE 4

15 EMOJIS have different numerical values. Put the values in the puzzle grid to agree the sum totals horizontally, vertically and diagonally.

Cross out numerical values when placed

↓ = ↻ Enter values when worked out   Yellow boxes are "given" values

1 x	🤏	=	
2 x	😐	=	2
1 x	☞	=	
2 x	❖	=	
2 x	✈	=	
2 x	✋	=	15
2 x	☹	=	
2 x	☺	=	
1 x	👍	=	21
2 x	💣	=	
2 x	⌘	=	1
1 x	🖕	=	10
2 x	🏳	=	
1 x	👎	=	
2 x	☠	=	

↘	↓	↓	↓	↓	↓	↙
→	🏳	✈	💣	😐	☹	55
→	⌘	🖕	🏳	✋	🤏	38
→	☺	💣	⌘	☠	☞	37
→	✋	👍	✈	😐	❖	71
→	☠	☹	👎	☺	❖	59
58	40	79	44	38	59	32

↘	↓	↓	↓	↓	↓	↙
→						55
→		10		15		38
→			1			37
→		21		2		71
→						59
58	40	79	44	38	59	32

1
2
3
5
6
7
8
10
11
14
15
16
18
19
21

Solution Overleaf

© Les Page 2020   ISBN 9781913565008   For more www.tarquingroup.com

EMOJIS

SOLUTION 4

↘	↓	↓	↓	↓	↓	↙
→	🏳	✈	💣	😐	🙁	55
→	⌘	☝	🏳	✋	☞	38
→	☺	💣	⌘	☠	☞	37
→	✋	👍	✈	😐	❖	71
→	☠	🙁	👇	☺	❖	59
58	40	79	44	38	59	32

↘	↓	↓	↓	↓	↓	↙
→	5	19	11	2	18	55
→	1	10	5	15	7	38
→	16	11	1	3	6	37
→	15	21	19	2	14	71
→	3	18	8	16	14	59
58	40	79	44	38	59	32

⌘	=	1
😐	=	2
☠	=	3
🏳	=	5
☞	=	6
☞	=	7
👇	=	8
☝	=	10
💣	=	11
❖	=	14
✋	=	15
☺	=	16
🙁	=	18
✈	=	19
👍	=	21

© Les Page 2020   ISBN 9781913565008

PUZZLE 5

15 EMOJIS have different numerical values. Put the values in the puzzle grid to agree the sum totals horizontally, vertically and diagonally.

Cross out numerical values when placed

↓ = ↻ Enter values when worked out   Yellow boxes are "given" values

1 x	🐭	=	3
2 x	😐	=	16
1 x	☞	=	
2 x	❖	=	
2 x	✈	=	10
2 x	✋	=	2
2 x	☹	=	
2 x	☺	=	
1 x	👍	=	
2 x	💣	=	
2 x	⌘	=	
1 x	☝	=	
2 x	⚑	=	
1 x	👎	=	1
2 x	☠	=	

↘	↓	↓	↓	↓	↓	↙
→	❖	☠	😐	💣	☺	74
→	☹	🐭	❖	👎	☞	41
→	✋	👍	😐	⌘	✈	47
→	☝	✈	☺	✋	⌘	44
→	☠	💣	⚑	⚑	☹	80
49	48	45	87	52	54	54

↘	↓	↓	↓	↓	↓	↙
→						74
→		3		1		41
→			16			47
→		10		2		44
→						80
49	48	45	87	52	54	54

1	
2	
3	
4	
6	
7	
8	
10	
11	
14	
15	
16	
17	
19	
21	

Solution Overleaf

© Les Page 2020   ISBN 9781913565008   For more www.tarquingroup.com

SOLUTION 5

↘	↓	↓	↓	↓	↓	↙
→	✥	☠	☺	💣	☺	74
→	☹	☞	✥	👎	☞	41
→	🖐	👍	☺	⌘	✈	47
→	☝	✈	☺	🖐	⌘	44
→	☠	💣	⚑	⚑	☹	80
49	48	45	87	52	54	54

↘	↓	↓	↓	↓	↓	↙
→	19	7	16	17	15	74
→	14	3	19	1	4	41
→	2	8	16	11	10	47
→	6	10	15	2	11	44
→	7	17	21	21	14	80
49	48	45	87	52	54	54

👎	=	1
🖐	=	2
☞	=	3
☞	=	4
☝	=	6
☠	=	7
👍	=	8
✈	=	10
⌘	=	11
☹	=	14
☺	=	15
☺	=	16
💣	=	17
✥	=	19
⚑	=	21

© Les Page 2020   ISBN 9781913565008

For more www.tarquingroup.com

EMOJIS

PUZZLE 6

15 EMOJIS have different numerical values. Put the values in the puzzle grid to agree the sum totals horizontally, vertically and diagonally.

Cross out numerical values when placed

↓ = ∩ Enter values when worked out   Yellow boxes are "given" values

1 x	🔭	=	7
2 x	😐	=	8
1 x	👉	=	
2 x	❖	=	
2 x	✈	=	
2 x	✋	=	12
2 x	🙁	=	
2 x	🙂	=	14
1 x	👍	=	
2 x	💣	=	
2 x	⌘	=	
1 x	☝	=	
2 x	🏳	=	
1 x	👎	=	
2 x	☠	=	15

↘	↓	↓	↓	↓	↓	↙
→	☝	✋	☠	👉	❖	57
→	🏳	☠	🙁	🔭	🙁	40
→	✈	💣	😐	🙂	⌘	71
→	👎	✋	✈	🙂	🏳	74
→	😐	👍	⌘	💣	❖	49
44	58	58	60	70	45	48

↘	↓	↓	↓	↓	↓	↙
→						57
→		15		7		40
→			8			71
→		12		14		74
→						49
44	58	58	60	70	45	48

2
3
4
7
8
9
10
12
13
14
15
16
18
19
20

Solution Overleaf

© Les Page 2020   ISBN 9781913565008   For more www.tarquingroup.com

SOLUTION 6

↘	↓	↓	↓	↓	↓	↙
→	☝	✋	☠	☞	✥	57
→	🏳	☠	☹	☞	☹	40
→	✈	💣	😐	☺	⌘	71
→	👎	✋	✈	☺	🏳	74
→	😐	👍	⌘	💣	✥	49
44	58	58	60	70	45	48

↘	↓	↓	↓	↓	↓	↙
→	2	12	15	19	9	57
→	10	15	4	7	4	40
→	20	16	8	14	13	71
→	18	12	20	14	10	74
→	8	3	13	16	9	49
44	58	58	60	70	45	48

☝	=	2
👍	=	3
☹	=	4
☞	=	7
😐	=	8
✥	=	9
🏳	=	10
✋	=	12
⌘	=	13
☺	=	14
☠	=	15
💣	=	16
👎	=	18
☞	=	19
✈	=	20

© Les Page 2020   ISBN 9781913565008

PUZZLE 7

15 EMOJIS have different numerical values. Put the values in the puzzle grid to agree the sum totals horizontally, vertically and diagonally.

Cross out numerical values when placed

↓ = ∩ Enter values when worked out   Yellow boxes are "given" values

1 x	🐦	=	
2 x	😐	=	
1 x	👉	=	11
2 x	❖	=	18
2 x	✈	=	21
2 x	✋	=	
2 x	☹	=	
2 x	☺	=	
1 x	👍	=	
2 x	💣	=	
2 x	⌘	=	9
1 x	☝	=	
2 x	🏳	=	
1 x	👎	=	
2 x	☠	=	20

↘	↓	↓	↓	↓	↓	↙
→	✈	🏳	⌘	✋	👎	65
→	💣	☠	☠	❖	🐦	68
→	😐	😐	👉	❖	☺	48
→	💣	⌘	☝	✈	☹	74
→	☺	☹	✋	👍	🏳	50
58	50	62	71	73	49	83

↘	↓	↓	↓	↓	↓	↙
→						65
→	20		18			68
→		11				48
→	9		21			74
→						50
58	50	62	71	73	49	83

2
4
6
7
8
9
10
11
12
13
17
18
19
20
21

Solution Overleaf

© Les Page 2020   ISBN 9781913565008

EMOJIS

SOLUTION 7

↘	↓	↓	↓	↓	↓	↙
→	✈	🏳	⌘	✋	👎	65
→	💣	☠	☠	❖	☞	68
→	😐	😐	☞	❖	☺	48
→	💣	⌘	☝	✈	☹	74
→	☺	☹	✋	👍	🏳	50
58	50	62	71	73	49	83

↘	↓	↓	↓	↓	↓	↙
→	21	10	9	12	13	65
→	8	20	20	18	2	68
→	6	6	11	18	7	48
→	8	9	19	21	17	74
→	7	17	12	4	10	50
58	50	62	71	73	49	83

Emoji		Value
☞	=	2
👍	=	4
😐	=	6
☺	=	7
💣	=	8
⌘	=	9
🏳	=	10
☞	=	11
✋	=	12
👎	=	13
☹	=	17
❖	=	18
☝	=	19
☠	=	20
✈	=	21

© Les Page 2020   ISBN 9781913565008

PUZZLE 8

15 EMOJIS have different numerical values. Put the values in the puzzle grid to agree the sum totals horizontally, vertically and diagonally.

Cross out numerical values when placed

↓ = ↱ Enter values when worked out   Yellow boxes are "given" values

1 x	🖇	=	
2 x	😐	=	6
1 x	☞	=	13
2 x	❖	=	12
2 x	✈	=	
2 x	✋	=	3
2 x	☹	=	
2 x	☺	=	
1 x	👍	=	
2 x	💣	=	
2 x	⌘	=	
1 x	☝	=	
2 x	⚑	=	21
1 x	👎	=	
2 x	☠	=	

↘	↓	↓	↓	↓	↓	↙
→	☝	☠	👍	💣	⚑	59
→	☹	☞	😐	✋	🖇	55
→	⌘	☺	⚑	❖	👎	74
→	☺	😐	☹	❖	✈	52
→	💣	✋	⌘	☠	✈	23
55	52	48	61	40	62	59

↘	↓	↓	↓	↓	↓	↙
→						59
→		13		3		55
→			21			74
→		6		12		52
→						23
55	52	48	61	40	62	59

2
3
4
5
6
9
11
12
13
14
15
17
18
19
21

Solution Overleaf

© Les Page 2020   ISBN 9781913565008   For more www.tarquingroup.com

EMOJIS

LEVEL H

SOLUTION 8

↘	↓	↓	↓	↓	↓	↙
→	☝	☠	👍	💣	🏳	59
→	☹	👉	😐	🖐	👈	55
→	⌘	☺	🏳	❖	👎	74
→	☺	😐	☹	❖	✈	52
→	💣	🖐	⌘	☠	✈	23
55	52	48	61	40	62	59

✈	=	2
🖐	=	3
💣	=	4
⌘	=	5
😐	=	6
☠	=	9
☝	=	11
❖	=	12
👉	=	13
👍	=	14
☹	=	15
☺	=	17
👈	=	18
👎	=	19
🏳	=	21

↘	↓	↓	↓	↓	↓	↙
→	11	9	14	4	21	59
→	15	13	6	3	18	55
→	5	17	21	12	19	74
→	17	6	15	12	2	52
→	4	3	5	9	2	23
55	52	48	61	40	62	59

© Les Page 2020   ISBN 9781913565008

For more www.tarquingroup.com

EMOJIS

PUZZLE 9

15 EMOJIS have different numerical values. Put the values in the puzzle grid to agree the sum totals horizontally, vertically and diagonally.

↓ = ∩ Enter values when worked out   Yellow boxes are "given" values

1 x	👆	=	
2 x	😐	=	18
1 x	👉	=	
2 x	❖	=	8
2 x	✈	=	5
2 x	✋	=	
2 x	☹	=	
2 x	☺	=	
1 x	👍	=	
2 x	💣	=	
2 x	⌘	=	
1 x	👆	=	
2 x	⚑	=	
1 x	👎	=	19
2 x	☠	=	16

↘	↓	↓	↓	↓	↓	↙
→	☹	☹	☺	⚑	👆	37
→	✈	☠	👆	👇	✋	47
→	😐	⚑	❖	👍	⌘	64
→	💣	😐	☺	✈	❖	54
→	💣	☠	✋	⌘	👉	68
69	74	73	19	62	42	51

↘	↓	↓	↓	↓	↓	↙
→						37
→		16		19		47
→			8			64
→		18		5		54
→						68
69	74	73	19	62	42	51

Cross out numerical values when placed

✗

1
2
3
5
6
7
8
9
13
14
16
17
18
19
21

Solution Overleaf

© Les Page 2020   ISBN 9781913565008   For more www.tarquingroup.com

SOLUTION 9

↘	↓	↓	↓	↓	↓	↙
→	☹	☹	☺	⚑	☞	37
→	✈	☠	☝	👎	✋	47
→	😐	⚑	❖	👍	⌘	64
→	💣	😐	☺	✈	❖	54
→	💣	☠	✋	⌘	☞	68
69	74	73	19	62	42	51

↘	↓	↓	↓	↓	↓	↙
→	9	9	2	14	3	37
→	5	16	6	19	1	47
→	18	14	8	7	17	64
→	21	18	2	5	8	54
→	21	16	1	17	13	68
69	74	73	19	62	42	51

✋	=	1
☺	=	2
☞	=	3
✈	=	5
☝	=	6
👍	=	7
❖	=	8
☹	=	9
☞	=	13
⚑	=	14
☠	=	16
⌘	=	17
😐	=	18
👎	=	19
💣	=	21

© Les Page 2020   ISBN 9781913565008

For more www.tarquingroup.com

PUZZLE 10

15 EMOJIS have different numerical values. Put the values in the puzzle grid to agree the sum totals horizontally, vertically and diagonally.

 Cross out numerical values when placed

↓ = ⌒ Enter values when worked out   Yellow boxes are "given" values

1 x	🐭	=	13
2 x	😊	=	
1 x	☞	=	
2 x	❖	=	3
2 x	✈	=	
2 x	✋	=	
2 x	☹	=	
2 x	☺	=	
1 x	👍	=	12
2 x	💣	=	
2 x	⌘	=	
1 x	☝	=	
2 x	🏳	=	
1 x	👎	=	20
2 x	☠	=	14

↘	↓	↓	↓	↓	↓	↙
→	⌘	☠	☺	❖	⌘	28
→	☝	👎	💣	☠	🏳	66
→	🏳	😐	☞	☹	💣	56
→	✈	❖	✋	👍	😐	43
→	☞	☺	☹	✋	✈	54
47	47	53	53	43	51	61

↘	↓	↓	↓	↓	↓	↙
→						28
→		20		14		66
→			13			56
→		3		12		43
→						54
47	47	53	53	43	51	61

1
3
4
6
7
8
9
11
12
13
14
15
16
17
20

Solution Overleaf

© Les Page 2020   ISBN 9781913565008   For more www.tarquingroup.com

SOLUTION 10

↘	↓	↓	↓	↓	↓	↙
→	⌘	☠	☺	❖	⌘	28
→	☝	👎	💣	☠	🏳	66
→	🏳	😐	👉	🙁	💣	56
→	✈	❖	✋	👍	😐	43
→	👉	☺	🙁	✋	✈	54
47	47	53	53	43	51	61

⌘	=	1
❖	=	3
☝	=	4
✋	=	6
😐	=	7
🙁	=	8
☺	=	9
🏳	=	11
👍	=	12
👉	=	13
☠	=	14
✈	=	15
👉	=	16
💣	=	17
👎	=	20

↘	↓	↓	↓	↓	↓	↙
→	1	14	9	3	1	28
→	4	20	17	14	11	66
→	11	7	13	8	17	56
→	15	3	6	12	7	43
→	16	9	8	6	15	54
47	47	53	53	43	51	61

PUZZLE 11

15 EMOJIS have different numerical values. Put the values in the puzzle grid to agree the sum totals horizontally, vertically and diagonally.

↓ = ↻ Enter values when worked out   Yellow boxes are "given" values

1 x	🐿	=	
2 x	😐	=	
1 x	☞	=	
2 x	❖	=	4
2 x	✈	=	
2 x	✋	=	
2 x	☹	=	6
2 x	☺	=	
1 x	👍	=	19
2 x	💣	=	10
2 x	⌘	=	8
1 x	☝	=	
2 x	⚑	=	
1 x	👎	=	
2 x	☠	=	

↘	↓	↓	↓	↓	↓	↙
→	⚑	⚑	😐	✈	👎	53
→	☝	⌘	☺	☹	☺	30
→	☠	☹	❖	❖	✈	35
→	⌘	💣	✋	👍	☞	41
→	☠	☞	💣	😐	✋	55
42	33	44	42	59	36	39

↘	↓	↓	↓	↓	↓	↙
→						53
→		8		6		30
→			4			35
→		10		19		41
→						55
42	33	44	42	59	36	39

1
2
3
4
5
6
7
8
9
10
12
13
15
18
19

Solution Overleaf

© Les Page 2020   ISBN 9781913565008   For more www.tarquingroup.com

EMOJIS

SOLUTION 11

↘	↓	↓	↓	↓	↓	↙
→	🏳	🏳	😐	✈	👎	53
→	☝	⌘	☺	☹	☺	30
→	☠	☹	❖	❖	✈	35
→	⌘	💣	✋	👍	☞	41
→	☠	☞	💣	😐	✋	55
42	33	44	42	59	36	39

☞	=	1
☝	=	2
✋	=	3
❖	=	4
🏳	=	5
☹	=	6
☺	=	7
⌘	=	8
☠	=	9
💣	=	10
✈	=	12
👎	=	13
☞	=	15
😐	=	18
👍	=	19

↘	↓	↓	↓	↓	↓	↙
→	5	5	18	12	13	53
→	2	8	7	6	7	30
→	9	6	4	4	12	35
→	8	10	3	19	1	41
→	9	15	10	18	3	55
42	33	44	42	59	36	39

EMOJIS

PUZZLE 12

15 EMOJIS have different numerical values. Put the values in the puzzle grid to agree the sum totals horizontally, vertically and diagonally.

↓ = ↺ Enter values when worked out   Yellow boxes are "given" values

Count	Emoji	=	Value
1 x	🐦	=	
2 x	😐	=	
1 x	👆	=	
2 x	❖	=	
2 x	✈	=	
2 x	✋	=	
2 x	☹	=	20
2 x	☺	=	
1 x	👍	=	
2 x	💣	=	19
2 x	⌘	=	2
1 x	☝	=	7
2 x	🏳	=	
1 x	👎	=	
2 x	☠	=	15

↘	↓	↓	↓	↓	↓	↙
→	👍	💣	✋	👆	✈	71
→	☠	☹	🏳	💣	☺	71
→	🏳	❖	⌘	☺	❖	45
→	✋	☠	😐	☝	✈	50
→	👆	😐	👎	☹	⌘	41
52	50	77	32	72	47	47

↘	↓	↓	↓	↓	↓	↙
→						71
→		20		19		71
→			2			45
→		15		7		50
→						41
52	50	77	32	72	47	47

Numerical values: 2, 4, 5, 6, 7, 8, 9, 10, 12, 13, 15, 16, 18, 19, 20

Solution Overleaf

© Les Page 2020   ISBN 9781913565008   For more www.tarquingroup.com

SOLUTION 12

↘	↓	↓	↓	↓	↓	↙
→	👍	💣	✋	☞	✈	71
→	☠	☹	🚩	💣	☺	71
→	🚩	❖	⌘	☺	❖	45
→	✋	☠	😐	☝	✈	50
→	👉	😐	👎	☹	⌘	41
52	50	77	32	72	47	47

↘	↓	↓	↓	↓	↓	↙
→	16	19	6	18	12	71
→	15	20	9	19	8	71
→	9	13	2	8	13	45
→	6	15	10	7	12	50
→	4	10	5	20	2	41
52	50	77	32	72	47	47

⌘	=	2
👉	=	4
👎	=	5
✋	=	6
☝	=	7
☺	=	8
🚩	=	9
😐	=	10
✈	=	12
❖	=	13
☠	=	15
👍	=	16
☞	=	18
💣	=	19
☹	=	20

© Les Page 2020   ISBN 9781913565008

EMOJIS

PUZZLE 13

15 EMOJIS have different numerical values. Put the values in the puzzle grid to agree the sum totals horizontally, vertically and diagonally.

Cross out numerical values when placed

↓ = ⋂ Enter values when worked out   Yellow boxes are "given" values

1 x	🐦	=	
2 x	😐	=	
1 x	👉	=	12
2 x	✦	=	13
2 x	✈	=	15
2 x	🖐	=	
2 x	☹	=	
2 x	☺	=	
1 x	👍	=	
2 x	💣	=	14
2 x	⌘	=	
1 x	☝	=	
2 x	🏳	=	8
1 x	👎	=	
2 x	☠	=	

↘	↓	↓	↓	↓	↓	↙
→	🖐	☠	👎	☹	☺	55
→	✦	🏳	😐	✦	☹	38
→	👍	🖐	👉	☝	🐦	69
→	☺	✈	💣	💣	😐	54
→	✈	⌘	🏳	☠	⌘	77
65	79	78	41	55	40	73

↘	↓	↓	↓	↓	↓	↙
→						55
→		8		13		38
→			12			69
→		15		14		54
→						77
65	79	78	41	55	40	73

1
3
6
7
8
9
10
12
13
14
15
16
19
20
21

Solution Overleaf

© Les Page 2020   ISBN 9781913565008   For more www.tarquingroup.com

SOLUTION 13

↘	↓	↓	↓	↓	↓	↙
→	🖐	☠	👎	☹	☺	55
→	❖	🏳	😐	❖	☹	38
→	👍	🖐	👉	☝	👉	69
→	☺	✈	💣	💣	😐	54
→	✈	⌘	🏳	☠	⌘	77
65	79	78	41	55	40	73

↘	↓	↓	↓	↓	↓	↙
→	20	16	6	3	10	55
→	13	8	1	13	3	38
→	21	20	12	9	7	69
→	10	15	14	14	1	54
→	15	19	8	16	19	77
65	79	78	41	55	40	73

Emoji		Value
😐	=	1
☹	=	3
👎	=	6
👉	=	7
🏳	=	8
☝	=	9
☺	=	10
👉	=	12
❖	=	13
💣	=	14
✈	=	15
☠	=	16
⌘	=	19
🖐	=	20
👍	=	21

© Les Page 2020   ISBN 9781913565008

EMOJIS

PUZZLE 14

15 EMOJIS have different numerical values. Put the values in the puzzle grid to agree the sum totals horizontally, vertically and diagonally.

Cross out numerical values when placed

↓ = ∩ Enter values when worked out   Yellow boxes are "given" values   ✗

1 x	👆(right)	=	
2 x	😐	=	7
1 x	👉	=	
2 x	❖	=	13
2 x	✈	=	
2 x	✋	=	
2 x	☹	=	
2 x	☺	=	15
1 x	👍	=	
2 x	💣	=	
2 x	⌘	=	
1 x	☝	=	3
2 x	🏳	=	
1 x	👎	=	
2 x	☠	=	8

Grid 1:

↘	↓	↓	↓	↓	↓	↙
→	👆	✋	😐	👉	✋	63
→	✈	☠	☠	☝	👍	40
→	✈	🏳	❖	🏳	☹	93
→	👎	😐	⌘	☺	💣	45
→	☺	☹	💣	⌘	❖	59
52	77	68	41	59	55	61

Grid 2:

↘	↓	↓	↓	↓	↓	↙
→						63
→		8		3		40
→			13			93
→		7		15		45
→						59
52	77	68	41	59	55	61

Values to cross out: 1, 3, 4, 7, 8, 9, 10, 12, 13, 14, 15, 16, 18, 20, 21

Solution Overleaf

© Les Page 2020   ISBN 9781913565008   For more www.tarquingroup.com

EMOJIS

SOLUTION 14

↘	↓	↓	↓	↓	↓	↙
→	👉	✋	😐	👉	✋	63
→	✈	☠	☠	☝	👍	40
→	✈	🚩	❖	🚩	☹	93
→	👎	😐	⌘	☺	💣	45
→	☺	☹	💣	⌘	❖	59
52	77	68	41	59	55	61

↘	↓	↓	↓	↓	↓	↙
→	12	14	7	16	14	63
→	20	8	8	3	1	40
→	20	21	13	21	18	93
→	10	7	4	15	9	45
→	15	18	9	4	13	59
52	77	68	41	59	55	61

👍	=	1
☝	=	3
⌘	=	4
😐	=	7
☠	=	8
💣	=	9
👎	=	10
👉	=	12
❖	=	13
✋	=	14
☺	=	15
👉	=	16
☹	=	18
✈	=	20
🚩	=	21

© Les Page 2020   ISBN 9781913565008

PUZZLE 15

15 EMOJIS have different numerical values. Put the values in the puzzle grid to agree the sum totals horizontally, vertically and diagonally.

Cross out numerical values when placed

↓ = ⌒ Enter values when worked out   Yellow boxes are "given" values

	↓	=	⌒
1 x	🖐	=	14
2 x	😐	=	3
1 x	👉	=	
2 x	❖	=	4
2 x	✈	=	
2 x	🖐	=	
2 x	🙁	=	
2 x	☺	=	11
1 x	👍	=	
2 x	💣	=	18
2 x	⌘	=	
1 x	☝	=	
2 x	🏳	=	
1 x	👎	=	
2 x	☠	=	

↘	↓	↓	↓	↓	↓	↙
→	🖐	👉	🏳	☺	🙁	66
→	👍	❖	🏳	🖐	✈	42
→	👎	☠	😐	⌘	✈	58
→	⌘	☺	🖐	💣	😐	55
→	💣	☠	❖	🙁	☝	65
66	54	64	40	79	49	38

↘	↓	↓	↓	↓	↓	↙
→						66
→		4		14		42
→			3			58
→		11		18		55
→						65
66	54	64	40	79	49	38

1
3
4
6
7
10
11
12
13
14
15
16
17
18
20

Solution Overleaf

© Les Page 2020   ISBN 9781913565008   For more www.tarquingroup.com

EMOJIS

SOLUTION 15

↘	↓	↓	↓	↓	↓	↙
→	🖐	☞	⚑	☺	☹	66
→	👍	❖	⚑	☜	✈	42
→	👎	☠	☺	⌘	✈	58
→	⌘	☺	🖐	💣	☺	55
→	💣	☠	❖	☹	☝	65
66	54	64	40	79	49	38

↘	↓	↓	↓	↓	↓	↙
→	7	15	13	11	20	66
→	1	4	13	14	10	42
→	12	17	3	16	10	58
→	16	11	7	18	3	55
→	18	17	4	20	6	65
66	54	64	40	79	49	38

👍	=	1
☺	=	3
❖	=	4
☝	=	6
🖐	=	7
✈	=	10
☺	=	11
👎	=	12
⚑	=	13
☜	=	14
☞	=	15
⌘	=	16
☠	=	17
💣	=	18
☹	=	20

© Les Page 2020   ISBN 9781913565008

PUZZLE 16

15 EMOJIS have different numerical values. Put the values in the puzzle grid to agree the sum totals horizontally, vertically and diagonally.

Cross out numerical values when placed

↓ = ⤴ Enter values when worked out   Yellow boxes are "given" values

1 x	☞	=	
2 x	😐	=	19
1 x	☞	=	
2 x	❖	=	
2 x	✈	=	
2 x	✋	=	
2 x	☹	=	11
2 x	☺	=	
1 x	👍	=	
2 x	💣	=	16
2 x	⌘	=	
1 x	☝	=	6
2 x	🏳	=	17
1 x	👎	=	
2 x	☠	=	

↘	↓	↓	↓	↓	↓	↙
→	❖	☞	💣	✈	✋	45
→	☠	💣	☠	☹	☺	58
→	☹	⌘	🏳	✈	✋	60
→	☞	😐	⌘	☝	👍	70
→	☺	🏳	😐	👎	❖	69
64	43	84	80	50	45	49

↘	↓	↓	↓	↓	↓	↙
→						45
→		16		11		58
→			17			60
→		19		6		70
→						69
64	43	84	80	50	45	49

2
4
5
6
8
10
11
12
13
15
16
17
19
20
21

Solution Overleaf

© Les Page 2020   ISBN 9781913565008   For more www.tarquingroup.com

SOLUTION 16

↘	↓	↓	↓	↓	↓	↙
→	✥	☞	💣	✈	🖐	45
→	☠	💣	☠	☹	☺	58
→	☹	⌘	🏳	✈	🖐	60
→	☞	😐	⌘	☝	👍	70
→	☺	🏳	😐	👎	✥	69
64	43	84	80	50	45	49

🖐	=	2
☞	=	4
✥	=	5
☝	=	6
☠	=	8
✈	=	10
☹	=	11
☞	=	12
👎	=	13
☺	=	15
💣	=	16
🏳	=	17
😐	=	19
⌘	=	20
👍	=	21

↘	↓	↓	↓	↓	↓	↙
→	5	12	16	10	2	45
→	8	16	8	11	15	58
→	11	20	17	10	2	60
→	4	19	20	6	21	70
→	15	17	19	13	5	69
64	43	84	80	50	45	49

© Les Page 2020   ISBN 9781913565008

PUZZLE 17

15 EMOJIS have different numerical values. Put the values in the puzzle grid to agree the sum totals horizontally, vertically and diagonally.

Cross out numerical values when placed

↓ = ↻ Enter values when worked out   Yellow boxes are "given" values

1 x	🖐	=	
2 x	😐	=	
1 x	👉	=	3
2 x	❖	=	1
2 x	✈	=	19
2 x	🖐	=	
2 x	☹	=	
2 x	☺	=	10
1 x	👍	=	
2 x	💣	=	
2 x	⌘	=	
1 x	☝	=	
2 x	🚩	=	6
1 x	👎	=	
2 x	☠	=	

↘	↓	↓	↓	↓	↓	↙
→	😐	🖐	☹	⌘	👍	65
→	❖	❖	💣	☺	✈	38
→	☹	☠	✈	🚩	☝	49
→	💣	🚩	😐	👉	🖐	28
→	🖐	⌘	☺	☠	👎	70
72	42	56	49	47	56	38

↘	↓	↓	↓	↓	↓	↙
→						65
→		1		10		38
→			19			49
→		6		3		28
→						70
72	42	56	49	47	56	38

Cross out column: 1, 2, 3, 4, 6, 7, 8, 9, 10, 11, 13, 15, 16, 19, 21

Solution Overleaf

© Les Page 2020   ISBN 9781913565008   For more www.tarquingroup.com

SOLUTION 17

↘	↓	↓	↓	↓	↓	↙
→	😐	🖐	☹	⌘	👍	65
→	❖	❖	💣	☺	✈	38
→	☹	☠	✈	🏳	☝	49
→	💣	🏳	😐	☞	👉	28
→	🖐	⌘	☺	☠	👎	70
72	42	56	49	47	56	38

↘	↓	↓	↓	↓	↓	↙
→	4	21	9	15	16	65
→	1	1	7	10	19	38
→	9	13	19	6	2	49
→	7	6	4	3	8	28
→	21	15	10	13	11	70
72	42	56	49	47	56	38

❖	=	1
☝	=	2
☞	=	3
😐	=	4
🏳	=	6
💣	=	7
👉	=	8
☹	=	9
☺	=	10
👎	=	11
☠	=	13
⌘	=	15
👍	=	16
✈	=	19
🖐	=	21

© Les Page 2020   ISBN 9781913565008

EMOJIS

LEVEL H

PUZZLE 18

15 EMOJIS have different numerical values. Put the values in the puzzle grid to agree the sum totals horizontally, vertically and diagonally.

Cross out numerical values when placed

↓ = ↺ Enter values when worked out   Yellow boxes are "given" values

Multiplier	Emoji	=	Value
1 x	🐌	=	
2 x	😐	=	
1 x	👆	=	8
2 x	✦	=	
2 x	✈	=	
2 x	✋	=	
2 x	☹	=	19
2 x	☺	=	11
1 x	👍	=	
2 x	💣	=	
2 x	⌘	=	
1 x	☝	=	
2 x	🚩	=	6
1 x	👎	=	
2 x	☠	=	2

Top grid:

↘	↓	↓	↓	↓	↓	↙
→	👆	✦	☺	😐	☝	60
→	💣	☹	☠	👆	💣	57
→	🚩	☹	🚩	✦	😐	45
→	✋	☺	👎	☠	⌘	37
→	✈	✋	⌘	👍	✈	78
63	65	74	31	45	62	60

Bottom grid:

↘	↓	↓	↓	↓	↓	↙
→						60
→		19		8		57
→			6			45
→		11		2		37
→						78
63	65	74	31	45	62	60

| 1 |
| 2 |
| 3 |
| 6 |
| 8 |
| 9 |
| 11 |
| 12 |
| 13 |
| 14 |
| 15 |
| 18 |
| 19 |
| 20 |
| 21 |

Solution Overleaf

© Les Page 2020   ISBN 9781913565008   For more www.tarquingroup.com

SOLUTION 18

↘	↓	↓	↓	↓	↓	↙
→	☞	❖	☺	☺	☝	60
→	💣	☹	☠	☞	💣	57
→	⚑	☹	⚑	❖	☺	45
→	✋	☺	👎	☠	⌘	37
→	✈	✋	⌘	👍	✈	78
63	65	74	31	45	62	60

☺	=	1
☠	=	2
👎	=	3
⚑	=	6
☞	=	8
⌘	=	9
☺	=	11
✋	=	12
❖	=	13
💣	=	14
☞	=	15
✈	=	18
☹	=	19
☝	=	20
👍	=	21

↘	↓	↓	↓	↓	↓	↙
→	15	13	11	1	20	60
→	14	19	2	8	14	57
→	6	19	6	13	1	45
→	12	11	3	2	9	37
→	18	12	9	21	18	78
63	65	74	31	45	62	60

© Les Page 2020   ISBN 9781913565008

EMOJIS

PUZZLE 19

15 EMOJIS have different numerical values. Put the values in the puzzle grid to agree the sum totals horizontally, vertically and diagonally.

Cross out numerical values when placed

↓	=	↰ Enter values when worked out		Yellow boxes are "given" values

		=	
1 x	🫳	=	
2 x	😐	=	4
1 x	👉	=	
2 x	❖	=	
2 x	✈	=	
2 x	✋	=	
2 x	☹	=	14
2 x	😊	=	12
1 x	👍	=	
2 x	💣	=	
2 x	⌘	=	10
1 x	☝	=	
2 x	🏳	=	
1 x	👎	=	
2 x	☠	=	9

↘	↓	↓	↓	↓	↓	↙
→	👍	🫳	✈	❖	🏳	67
→	🏳	😊	✋	☠	☝	41
→	❖	😐	⌘	☹	☠	54
→	✈	😐	✋	☹	😊	58
→	💣	💣	👉	⌘	👎	75
55	72	57	64	64	38	44

↘	↓	↓	↓	↓	↓	↙
→						67
→		12		9		41
→			10			54
→		4		14		58
→						75
55	72	57	64	64	38	44

Cross out numerical values: 1, 3, 4, 5, 8, 9, 10, 11, 12, 14, 16, 17, 18, 20, 21

Solution Overleaf

© Les Page 2020   ISBN 9781913565008
For more www.tarquingroup.com

EMOJIS

SOLUTION 19

↘	↓	↓	↓	↓	↓	↙
→	👍	☞	✈	❖	⚑	67
→	⚑	☺	✋	☠	☝	41
→	❖	😐	⌘	☹	☠	54
→	✈	😐	✋	☹	☺	58
→	💣	💣	☞	⌘	👎	75
55	72	57	64	64	38	44

☝	=	1
👍	=	3
😐	=	4
👎	=	5
✋	=	8
☠	=	9
⌘	=	10
⚑	=	11
☺	=	12
☹	=	14
☞	=	16
❖	=	17
☞	=	18
✈	=	20
💣	=	21

↘	↓	↓	↓	↓	↓	↙
→	3	16	20	17	11	67
→	11	12	8	9	1	41
→	17	4	10	14	9	54
→	20	4	8	14	12	58
→	21	21	18	10	5	75
55	72	57	64	64	38	44

© Les Page 2020   ISBN 9781913565008   For more www.tarquingroup.com

PUZZLE 20

15 EMOJIS have different numerical values. Put the values in the puzzle grid to agree the sum totals horizontally, vertically and diagonally.

Cross out numerical values when placed

↓ = ⤴ Enter values when worked out   Yellow boxes are "given" values

1 x	🐭	=	
2 x	😐	=	6
1 x	👉	=	
2 x	❖	=	
2 x	✈	=	
2 x	✋	=	
2 x	☹	=	2
2 x	☺	=	9
1 x	👍	=	
2 x	💣	=	
2 x	⌘	=	
1 x	☝	=	17
2 x	🚩	=	
1 x	👎	=	18
2 x	☠	=	

↘	↓	↓	↓	↓	↓	↙
→	❖	☠	✋	⌘	💣	51
→	👍	👎	✋	☹	💣	35
→	🚩	⌘	😐	☹	❖	44
→	✈	☺	😐	☝	☺	55
→	☠	🚩	👉	✈	🐭	72
40	50	75	37	56	39	57

↘	↓	↓	↓	↓	↓	↙
→						51
→		18		2		35
→			6			44
→		9		17		55
→						72
40	50	75	37	56	39	57

2
3
4
5
6
7
9
11
12
14
16
17
18
19
21

Solution Overleaf

© Les Page 2020   ISBN 9781913565008

For more www.tarquingroup.com

SOLUTION 20

↘	↓	↓	↓	↓	↓	↙
→	✦	☠	✋	⌘	💣	51
→	👍	👎	✋	☹	💣	35
→	🏳	⌘	😐	☹	✦	44
→	✈	☺	😐	☝	☺	55
→	☠	🏳	👉	✈	👉	72
40	50	75	37	56	39	57

☹	=	2
✋	=	3
✦	=	4
👍	=	5
😐	=	6
💣	=	7
☺	=	9
🏳	=	11
👉	=	12
✈	=	14
☠	=	16
☝	=	17
👎	=	18
👉	=	19
⌘	=	21

↘	↓	↓	↓	↓	↓	↙
→	4	16	3	21	7	51
→	5	18	3	2	7	35
→	11	21	6	2	4	44
→	14	9	6	17	9	55
→	16	11	19	14	12	72
40	50	75	37	56	39	57

© Les Page 2020   ISBN 9781913565008   For more www.tarquingroup.com

PUZZLE 21

15 EMOJIS have different numerical values. Put the values in the puzzle grid to agree the sum totals horizontally, vertically and diagonally.

Cross out numerical values when placed

↓ = ↩ Enter values when worked out   Yellow boxes are "given" values

Count	Emoji	=	Value
1 x	🐦	=	
2 x	😐	=	13
1 x	👉	=	
2 x	✳	=	21
2 x	✈	=	
2 x	✋	=	5
2 x	🙁	=	
2 x	☺	=	
1 x	👍	=	14
2 x	💣	=	
2 x	⌘	=	
1 x	☝	=	
2 x	🏳	=	6
1 x	👎	=	
2 x	☠	=	

Values to cross out: 1, 3, 5, 6, 8, 9, 10, 12, 13, 14, 16, 17, 18, 19, 21

Grid 1:

↘	↓	↓	↓	↓	↓	↙
→	🏳	✋	👎	🙁	⌘	42
→	☝	✳	✈	😐	☠	68
→	✳	👉	✋	👉	💣	62
→	✈	👍	😐	🏳	☠	51
→	🙁	😐	⌘	💣	🙁	54
53	65	44	56	57	55	50

Grid 2:

↘	↓	↓	↓	↓	↓	↙
→						42
→	21		13			68
→		5				62
→	14		6			51
→						54
53	65	44	56	57	55	50

Solution Overleaf

© Les Page 2020   ISBN 9781913565008   For more www.tarquingroup.com

SOLUTION 21

↘	↓	↓	↓	↓	↓	↙
→	⚑	✋	👎	☺	⌘	42
→	☝	❖	✈	😐	☠	68
→	❖	👉	✋	👉	💣	62
→	✈	👍	😐	⚑	☠	51
→	🙁	☺	⌘	💣	🙁	54
53	65	44	56	57	55	50

↘	↓	↓	↓	↓	↓	↙
→	6	5	19	3	9	42
→	16	21	10	13	8	68
→	21	1	5	17	18	62
→	10	14	13	6	8	51
→	12	3	9	18	12	54
53	65	44	56	57	55	50

👉	=	1
☺	=	3
✋	=	5
⚑	=	6
☠	=	8
⌘	=	9
✈	=	10
🙁	=	12
😐	=	13
👍	=	14
☝	=	16
👉	=	17
💣	=	18
👎	=	19
❖	=	21

© Les Page 2020   ISBN 9781913565008   For more www.tarquingroup.com

EMOJIS

LEVEL H

PUZZLE 22

15 EMOJIS have different numerical values. Put the values in the puzzle grid to agree the sum totals horizontally, vertically and diagonally.

↓ = ⤴ Enter values when worked out   Yellow boxes are "given" values

Cross out numerical values when placed

	emoji	=	value
1 x	💣👉	=	
2 x	😐	=	20
1 x	👉	=	
2 x	✣	=	6
2 x	✈	=	
2 x	✋	=	7
2 x	☹	=	3
2 x	☺	=	
1 x	👍	=	
2 x	💣	=	2
2 x	⌘	=	
1 x	☝	=	
2 x	⚑	=	
1 x	👎	=	
2 x	☠	=	

↘	↓	↓	↓	↓	↓	↙
→	😐	☠	✣	⚑	⌘	54
→	☺	✋	✈	✣	👎	42
→	👍	👉	☹	✋	☝	33
→	☹	😐	👉	💣	✈	54
→	☺	☠	⚑	⌘	💣	46
59	68	56	42	33	30	34

↘	↓	↓	↓	↓	↓	↙
→						54
→		7		6		42
→			3			33
→		20		2		54
→						46
59	68	56	42	33	30	34

1
2
3
4
5
6
7
8
9
10
13
14
16
20
21

© Les Page 2020   ISBN 9781913565008   For more www.tarquingroup.com

SOLUTION 22

↘	↓	↓	↓	↓	↓	↙
→	😐	☠	❖	⚑	⌘	54
→	☺	✋	✈	❖	👎	42
→	👍	👈	☹	✋	☝	33
→	☹	😐	👉	💣	✈	54
→	☺	☠	⚑	⌘	💣	46
59	68	56	42	33	30	34

↘	↓	↓	↓	↓	↓	↙
→	20	10	6	4	14	54
→	16	7	8	6	5	42
→	13	9	3	7	1	33
→	3	20	21	2	8	54
→	16	10	4	14	2	46
59	68	56	42	33	30	34

☝	=	1
💣	=	2
☹	=	3
⚑	=	4
👎	=	5
❖	=	6
✋	=	7
✈	=	8
👈	=	9
☠	=	10
👍	=	13
⌘	=	14
☺	=	16
😐	=	20
👉	=	21

© Les Page 2020   ISBN 9781913565008

PUZZLE 23

15 EMOJIS have different numerical values. Put the values in the puzzle grid to agree the sum totals horizontally, vertically and diagonally.

Cross out numerical values when placed

↓ = ∩ Enter values when worked out   Yellow boxes are "given" values

1 x	🐦	=	
2 x	😐	=	
1 x	☞	=	2
2 x	❖	=	
2 x	✈	=	
2 x	✋	=	4
2 x	☹	=	17
2 x	☺	=	
1 x	👍	=	
2 x	💣	=	8
2 x	⌘	=	
1 x	☝	=	
2 x	⚑	=	
1 x	👎	=	
2 x	☠	=	1

↘	↓	↓	↓	↓	↓	↙
→	✈	⚑	❖	🐦	✋	41
→	⌘	☹	😐	☞	☺	63
→	☠	☺	✋	✈	❖	44
→	😐	☠	💣	💣	☹	53
→	👎	⌘	👍	☝	⚑	49
14	42	48	61	46	53	46

↘	↓	↓	↓	↓	↓	↙
→						41
→		17		2		63
→			4			44
→		1		8		53
→						49
14	42	48	61	46	53	46

1
2
3
4
5
7
8
9
11
12
13
17
18
19
21

Solution Overleaf

© Les Page 2020   ISBN 9781913565008   For more www.tarquingroup.com

SOLUTION 23

↘	↓	↓	↓	↓	↓	↙
→	✈	🏳	❖	☞	🖐	41
→	⌘	☹	😐	☞	☺	63
→	☠	☺	🖐	✈	❖	44
→	😐	☠	💣	💣	☹	53
→	👎	⌘	👍	☝	🏳	49
14	42	48	61	46	53	46

↘	↓	↓	↓	↓	↓	↙
→	12	5	9	11	4	41
→	7	17	19	2	18	63
→	1	18	4	12	9	44
→	19	1	8	8	17	53
→	3	7	21	13	5	49
14	42	48	61	46	53	46

☠	=	1
☞	=	2
👎	=	3
🖐	=	4
🏳	=	5
⌘	=	7
💣	=	8
❖	=	9
☜	=	11
✈	=	12
☝	=	13
☹	=	17
☺	=	18
😐	=	19
👍	=	21

© Les Page 2020   ISBN 9781913565008

PUZZLE

The 15 letters in **NIGHTMARE BLOCKS** have different numerical values. Place values to agree sum totals horizontally, vertically and diagonally.

Cross out numerical values when placed

↓ = ∩ Enter values when worked out Green boxes are "given" values

Letter	=	Value
N	=	
I	=	1
G	=	14
H	=	17
T	=	20
M	=	
A	=	21
R	=	
E	=	9
B	=	
L	=	
O	=	
C	=	5
K	=	
S	=	

↘	↓	↓	↓	↓	↓	↙
→	N	I	R	B	M	40
→	K	E	E	A	L	52
→	S	B	H	I	C	46
→	N	T	R	G	O	59
→	G	A	M	H	T	79
79	52	62	59	64	39	68

↘	↓	↓	↓	↓	↓	↙
→		1				40
→	9	9	21			52
→			17	1	5	46
→				14		59
→	14	21		17	20	79
79	52	62	59	64	39	68

Values: 1, 3, 4, 5, 7, 8, 9, 10, 11, 12, 13, 14, 17, 20, 21

Solution Overleaf

© Les Page 2020 A preview of another Les Page title *Nightmare Blocks - Starter* for details see page 3 or visit www.tarquingroup.com

SOLUTION

↘	↓	↓	↓	↓	↓	↙
→	N	I	R	B	M	40
→	K	E	E	A	L	52
→	S	B	H	I	C	46
→	N	T	R	G	O	59
→	G	A	M	H	T	79
79	52	62	59	64	39	68

I	=	1
L	=	3
O	=	4
C	=	5
M	=	7
N	=	8
E	=	9
K	=	10
B	=	11
S	=	12
R	=	13
G	=	14
H	=	17
T	=	20
A	=	21

↘	↓	↓	↓	↓	↓	↙
→	8	1	13	11	7	40
→	10	9	9	21	3	52
→	12	11	17	1	5	46
→	8	20	13	14	4	59
→	14	21	7	17	20	79
79	52	62	59	64	39	68

PUZZLE

YOU WILL NEVER ESCAPE "DOING TIME" ON THIS PUZZLE !

Every block MUST contain 1, 2, 3 & 4 in the left hand column and 1 to 32 MUST be placed in the centre columns to agree the totals.

Cross out numerical values when placed

1	2	3
4	5	6
7	8	9
10	11	12
13	14	15
16	17	16
19	20	21
22	23	24
25	26	27
28	29	30
31	32	☺

Block 1:

1	+		=	29
	+		=	12
	+		=	16
3	+		=	26

Block 2:

2	+		=	24
	+		=	4
	+		=	14
	+		=	26

Block 3:

3	+		=	14
	+		=	3
	+		=	17
	+		=	23

Block 4:

3	+		=	29
	+		=	22
	+		=	25
2	+		=	8

Block 5:

4	+		=	33
	+		=	11
1	+		=	8
	+		=	15

Block 6:

4	+		=	31
	+		=	23
	+		=	6
	+		=	32

Block 7:

2	+		=	18
	+		=	32
	+		=	8
	+		=	22

Block 8:

2	+		=	34
	+		=	21
3	+		=	18
	+		=	4

Solution Overleaf

© Les Page 2020 A preview of another Les Page title *The Compendium* - for details see page 3 or visit www.tarquingroup.com

SOLUTION

LOOK ! ↘ HAVING "DONE TIME" PROVES IT CAN BE SOLVED ! 👌 ☺

1	+	28	=	29
4	+	8	=	12
2	+	14	=	16
3	+	23	=	26

2	+	22	=	24
3	+	1	=	4
4	+	10	=	14
1	+	25	=	26

3	+	11	=	14
1	+	2	=	3
4	+	13	=	17
2	+	21	=	23

3	+	26	=	29
4	+	18	=	22
1	+	24	=	25
2	+	6	=	8

4	+	29	=	33
2	+	9	=	11
1	+	7	=	8
3	+	12	=	15

4	+	27	=	31
3	+	20	=	23
1	+	5	=	6
2	+	30	=	32

2	+	16	=	18
1	+	31	=	32
4	+	4	=	8
3	+	19	=	22

2	+	32	=	34
4	+	17	=	21
3	+	15	=	18
1	+	3	=	4

© Les Page 2020 A preview of another Les Page title *The Compendium* - for details see page 3 or visit www.tarquingroup.com

PUZZLE

THE TWO - WAY MULTIPLICATION PUZZLE.

A × B = ↓			☺	B × C = ↓	Numbers in columns A, B & C on the right must be put in the puzzle so that A × B = the totals on the left & B × C equal the totals on the right.	For each column, cross out numbers as you enter - note they are not in order. ↓ ↓ ↓		
↓	A	B	C	↓	Scribble area	A	B	C
10				12		1	1	3
45				25		1	2	4
16				16		2	2	4
32				32		2	2	4
54				30		2	3	4
12				12		4	3	5
6				12		4	3	5
18				12		5	4	6
8				56		5	5	6
4				18		5	5	7
5				35		6	6	7
2				3		8	7	8
35				63		9	8	9
20				24		9	8	9

Solution Overleaf

© Les Page 2020 A preview of another Les Page title *The Compendium* - for details see page 3 or visit www.tarquingroup.com

SOLUTION

A		B
×	↓	×
B	👍	C
=	☺	=
↓		↓

↓	A	B	C	↓
10	5	2	6	12
45	9	5	5	25
16	8	2	8	16
32	4	8	4	32
54	9	6	5	30
12	4	3	4	12
6	2	3	4	12
18	6	3	4	12
8	1	8	7	56
4	2	2	9	18
5	1	5	7	35
2	2	1	3	3
35	5	7	9	63
20	5	4	6	24

© Les Page 2020 A preview of another Les Page title *The Compendium* - for details see page 3 or visit www.tarquingroup.com

PUZZLE
WHAT'S IN STORE HERE ?

A warehouse has 25 large rooms. Each room has six storage areas numbered from 1 to 6. Each room has interlinking glass doors to other rooms. The storage areas adjacent to the interlinking glass doors have the same storage area number as shown in the example below:

6	or	4	4
6			

↖   ↗
interlinking
glass doors

Your challenge is to insert the missing storage area numbers so that each room contains storage area numbers from 1 to 6.

3	5	1
1	5	2
4	3	6
5	3	2

The warehouse grid:

		2	5		
4		3			1		2
1		2	4	6			5
2							4
5		4		2			5
6							3
2		5		4			5
3							6
1		6		5			4
4							2
6		1		3			5
1			4				1
3		5		2			3
2							2
5		3			5		6
3			4				3
2		5		6			5
		2	3		

Solution Overleaf

© Les Page 2020 A preview of another Les Page title *The Compendium* - for details see page 3 or visit www.tarquingroup.com

SOLUTION

LOOK ! ↘ HAVING "DONE TIME" PROVES IT CAN BE SOLVED ! ✆ ☺

			6	2	5			
4	5	3	3	4	1	1	4	2
1	6	2	2	4	6	6	3	5
2	6	3	3	5	1	1	3	4
5	1	4	4	5	2	2	6	5
6	1	3	3	6	1	1	6	3
2	4	5	5	6	4	4	2	5
3	4	2	2	1	3	3	2	6
1	5	6	6	1	5	5	1	4
4	5	3	3	2	4	4	1	2
6	2	1	1	2	3	3	6	5
1	2	4	4	6	5	5	6	1
3	6	5	5	6	2	2	4	3
2	6	4	4	1	3	3	4	2
5	1	3	3	1	5	5	1	6
3	1	6	6	4	2	2	1	3
2	4	5	5	4	6	6	4	5
			2	3	1			

© Les Page 2020 A preview of another Les Page title *The Compendium* - for details see page 3 or visit www.tarquingroup.com

PUZZLE

AT FIRST GLANCE IT MAY LOOK IMPOSSIBLE TO DO! ☹
BUT USING YOUR INITATIVE IT CAN BE DONE! NEVER GIVE UP. ✍

PLACE THESE 33 NUMBERS CORRECTLY TO SOLVE THIS PUZZLE

2	10	12	17	18	22	24	27	28	33	34
36	40	43	46	55	63	67	75	78	79	92
96	110	112	112	123	132	150	178	207	228	270

Just plus... that's all you've got to do!

```
16  +  [  ]  =  [  ]  +  [  ]  =  [  ]  +  19  =  [  ]
 +      +        +        +        +        +       +
[  ]  +  [  ]  =  76  +  20  =  [  ]  +  [  ]  =  [  ]
 =      =        =        =        =        =       =
59  +  51  =  [  ]  +  [  ]  =  [  ]  +  [  ]  =  [  ]
 +      +        +        +        +        +       +
[  ]  +  [  ]  =  [  ]  +  35  =  [  ]  +  [  ]  =  [  ]
 =      =        =        =        =        =       =
71  +  [  ]  =  [  ]  +  57  =  [  ]  +  [  ]  =  [  ]
 +      +        +        +        +        +       +
41  +  37  =  [  ]  +  [  ]  =  88  +  [  ]  =  [  ]
 =      =        =        =        =        =       =
[  ]  +  116  =  [  ]  +  [  ]  =  295  +  87  =  382
```

Solution Overleaf

© Les Page 2020 A preview of another Les Page title *The Compendium* - for details see page 3 or visit www.tarquingroup.com

SOLUTION

INITATIVE USED.

IT CAN BE DONE !

🖐

☺

EVERYTHING ADDED = THE TOTALS !

16	+	18	=	34	+	2	=	36	+	19	=	55
+		+		+		+		+		+		+
43	+	33	=	76	+	20	=	96	+	27	=	123
=		=		=		=		=		=		=
51	+	59	=	110	+	22	=	132	+	46	=	178
+		+		+		+		+		+		+
12	+	28	=	40	+	35	=	75	+	17	=	92
=		=		=		=		=		=		=
71	+	79	=	150	+	57	=	207	+	63	=	270
+		+		+		+		+		+		+
41	+	37	=	78	+	10	=	88	+	24	=	112
=		=		=		=		=		=		=
112	+	116	=	228	+	67	=	295	+	87	=	382

© Les Page 2020 A preview of another Les Page title *The Compendium* - for details see page 3 or visit www.tarquingroup.com

Scribble Page

Need a New Tarquin Challenge?

We have a series of number and logic puzzles for a variety of ages and skill levels. See all at our website - but here are a selection:

 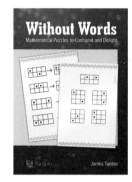 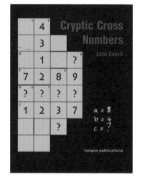

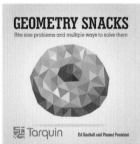  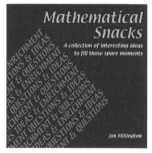

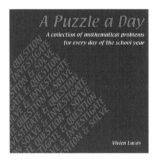 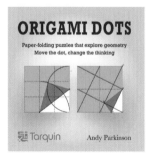 

Bestselling titles like Without Words, Geometry Snacks and A Puzzle a Day will be joined by Birds, Bees and Burgers in 2021.

Buy Tarquin books in most trade outlets or from www.tarquingroup.com